The
FRENCH
Kitchen Cookbook

First published in 2012

LOVE FOOD is an imprint of Parragon Books Ltd

Parragon
Queen Street House
4 Queen Street
Bath BA1 1HE, UK

ISBN: 978-1-4454-7857-9

Printed in China

Design by Tracy Killick
New photography by Clive Streeter
New food styling by Teresa Goldfinch

Notes for the reader

This book uses standard kitchen measuring spoons and cups. All spoon and cup measurements are level unless otherwise indicated. Unless otherwise stated, milk is assumed to be whole, eggs are large, individual vegetables are medium, and pepper is freshly ground black pepper. Unless otherwise stated, all root vegetables should be washed and peeled before using.

Garnishes and serving suggestions are all optional and not necessarily included in the recipe ingredients or method. The times given are only an approximate guide. Preparation times differ according to the techniques used by different people and the cooking times may also vary from those given. Optional ingredients, variations, or serving suggestions have not been included in the calculations.

Recipes using raw or very lightly cooked eggs should be avoided by infants, the elderly, pregnant women, and people with weakened immune systems. Pregnant and breast-feeding women are advised to avoid eating peanuts and peanut products. People with nut allergies should be aware that some of the prepared ingredients used in the recipes in this book may contain nuts. Always check the packaging before use.

Picture acknowledgments

The publisher would like to thank the following for permission to reproduce copyright material on the following pages:

Linen backgrounds, textured borders, and decorative frames (throughout): Fotolia/Tombaky; CG Textures; Fotolia/Robynmac.

Contents

Introduction

The French—be they young or old, sophisticated urbanites or rural agricultural workers—have a special place in their hearts for the unpretentious, hearty, and satisfying food that epitomizes their national cuisine. French food showcases the best of fresh, seasonal ingredients and is inevitably accompanied by a good selection of wines.

To complement a delicious French meal, it's important to capture the relaxed ambience that is associated with all good bistros, brasseries, and, indeed, home-cooked meals in France. The iconic image of a cozy neighborhood restaurant, with a zinc-topped bar, paper or checkered tablecloths, flickering candlelight, and the daily specials displayed on chalkboards may not be exactly right for everyday eating, but you can certainly capture charming buzz of playful conversation that accompanies great cooking in France.

Traditional, home-style dishes, such as Coq au Vin, Cassoulet, Boeuf Bourguinon, Soupe à l'Oignon and Croque-Monsieur, with their solid roots on bistro menus throughout the country will become a much-loved part of your own repertoire.

It is the simplicity of French food that makes it ideal for re-creating at home. As you look through this beautifully photographed collection of tempting recipes, you will find familiar ingredients and basic cooking techniques. This is not the food of Michelin-starred kitchens—it is food to enjoy with family and friends.

Bon appétit!

PAIN DE CAMPAGNE
POIDS PRIX   PRIX
       AU KG   PIECE
1KG2G 2.37   2.85

chapter one

Appetizers

Soupe de poissons
Fish Soup

❖ **Serves 6–8**
❖ **Prepared in 20–30 minutes,**
   plus chilling and standing
❖ **Cooks in 1½ hours**

3½ cups olive oil
3 onions, coarsely chopped
3 carrots, coarsely chopped
3 celery stalks, coarsely chopped
1 fennel bulb, finely chopped
6 garlic cloves, coarsely chopped
1 bay leaf
⅔ cup Vermouth
2 thyme sprigs
2¼ pounds whole fish, such as sea bass or
   pollock, gutted, filleted, but bones reserved

1 pound bones from white fish
8 ounces unpeeled shrimp
10 cups water
juice and zest of 1 orange
pinch of saffron
toasted slices of baguette and grated
   Parmesan cheese, to serve
salt and pepper

Rouille
½ cup fresh bread crumbs soaked in
   1 tablespoon water
3 garlic cloves, coarsely chopped
1 egg yolk
1 red chile, seeded and chopped
½ teaspoon salt
1 cup olive oil

one Place a large saucepan over medium heat and add the olive oil. Add the onions, carrots, celery, fennel, garlic, and bay leaf and cook gently for 20 minutes, or until soft. Add the Vermouth and thyme and simmer for 2 minutes. Add the fish, fish bones, and shrimp and increase the heat. Cook, stirring, for 5 minutes, then add the water, orange juice and zest, and saffron. Bring to a boil and simmer for 45 minutes. Remove the bay leaf.

two Meanwhile, make the rouille. Put all of the ingredients except for the olive oil into a food processor and process to a paste. Keep blending and add the olive oil in a slow stream until the consistency is that of a thick mayonnaise. Put in the refrigerator to chill.

three Crush the fish bones by processing the soup, in batches, in a food processor or blender. Let stand for 20 minutes. Strain through a colander first, then through a fine strainer, then pour into a saucepan. Season with salt and pepper and reheat again to serve.

four Serve immediately with slices of toasted baguette topped with grated Parmesan cheese and bowls of rouille alongside.

Potage St Germain

Pea Soup

✤ Serves 4
✤ Prepared in
  15–20 minutes
✤ Cooks in 20–30 minutes

3 tablespoons butter
¼ cup finely chopped shallots
4 cups vegetable stock or water
2¾ cups shelled peas
pinch of sugar
¼ cup crème fraîche
salt and pepper
croutons and blue cheese,
  such as Roquefort, crumbled,
  to serve

one

two

two

one Melt the butter in a large saucepan over medium heat. Add the shallots and sauté, stirring, for 2–3 minutes, or until soft. Add the stock, peas, and sugar, season with salt and pepper, and bring to a boil, uncovered. Simmer for 15–20 minutes, or until the peas are tender.

Two Strain the peas and reserve the cooking liquid. Process the peas in a food processor or blender, then return the puree to the pan. Gradually stir in the cooking liquid until you have the desired consistency.

Three Reheat the soup. Stir in the crème fraîche and adjust the seasoning. Serve immediately with croutons and blue cheese sprinkled over the soup.

Rillettes de porc

Potted Pork

* ❖ Makes about 3¼ pounds
* ❖ Prepared in 15–20 minutes
* ❖ Cooks in 4–6 hours

1 pound pork shoulder
2¼ pounds pork belly, rindless and boneless
1½ cups pork fat or lard
2 cups water
1 bouquet garni of 2 thyme sprigs, 2 parsley
   sprigs, and 3 bay leaves, tied with string
1 clove

½ teaspoon allspice
grating of fresh nutmeg
salt and pepper

To serve
pickles
mustard
baguette, sliced in half, rubbed with garlic
   halves, and toasted

one Cut the meat into 2-inch cubes and chop the fat into ½-inch cubes. Place the meat and fat in a large, heavy saucepan with the water, bouquet garni, and clove. Don't be tempted to add any more water—this method is a type of gentle steaming.

Two Cover the pan and place it over the lowest heat your stove can create, using a heat diffuser if you've got one, or place it into a low oven at 250°F. Cook for 4–6 hours, checking and stirring about every 30 minutes to make sure that it's not burning. Remove from the heat and set aside to cool. Remove the bouquet garni and clove. While it's still slightly warm, add the spices and season with salt and pepper, then take two forks and gently tear apart the pork, mixing the fat with the meat. Be careful to keep the texture and avoid turning the meat into a paste.

three Cover the meat with a piece of wax paper or plastic wrap and refrigerate for 2–3 days before serving (although you could eat it right away). It will last for at least an additional week in the refrigerator, but if you put it into sterilized jars and spread a layer of melted lard on top, it will keep for months. To serve, drop a spoonful onto a plate beside some pickles, mustard, and a baguette half.

Quiches lorraines
Quiche Lorraine Tarts

❖ **Makes 6 quiches**
❖ **Prepared in**
   20–30 minutes
❖ **Cooks in 40–50 minutes**

9 ounces of store-bought
   rolled dough pie crust
all-purpose flour, for dusting
⅔ cup unsmoked lard leaves
   or diced ham
2 extra-large eggs
1 cup whipping cream
1 cup shredded Gruyère cheese
   or Swiss cheese
grating of fresh nutmeg
salt and pepper

one Remove the dough from the refrigerator about 10 minutes before you roll it out and preheat the oven to 400°F with a baking sheet inside.

Two Divide the dough into six equal pieces and roll out each on a lightly floured surface into 6–7-inch circles. Use to line six 4½-inch tart pans, leaving the excess dough hanging over the edges. Line the dough with parchment paper and fill with pie weights or dried beans. Put the tart pans on the hot baking sheet and bake in the oven for 5 minutes, or until the rim is set. Remove the paper and weights, then return the tart shells to the oven and bake for an additional 5 minutes, or until the bottoms look dry. Remove the tart shells from the oven and let cool on the baking sheet. Reduce the oven temperature to 375°F.

Three Meanwhile, put the lard leaves in a skillet over low heat and sauté for 3 minutes, or until the fat begins to melt. Increase the heat to medium and continue sautéeing until they are crisp. (Omit this step if you are using diced ham.)

four Sprinkle the lard leaves or ham over the pastry shell. Beat together the eggs, cream, and cheese, then season with the salt, pepper, and nutmeg. Carefully divide the filling among the pastry shells, then return the tarts to the oven to bake for 20–25 minutes, or until the filling is set and the pastry is golden brown. Transfer the quiches to a wire rack to cool completely, trim the excess pastry before sewing.

Two

three

four

Salade niçoise
Tuna, Egg & Olive Salad

✤ Serves 4–6
✤ Prepared in 20–25 minutes
✤ Cooks in 10–15 minutes

2 tuna steaks, about ¼ inch thick
olive oil, for brushing
2½ cups green beans, trimmed

garlic vinaigrette
2 hearts of lettuce, leaves separated
3 extra-large hard-boiled eggs, quartered
2 juicy vine-ripened tomatoes,
   cut into wedges
1 (2-ounce) can anchovy fillets in oil, drained
½ cup Niçoise olives (or ripe black olives)
salt and pepper

one Heat a ridged grill pan over high heat until you can feel the heat rising from the surface. Brush the tuna steaks with oil on one side, place oiled-side down on the hot pan, and grill for 2 minutes.

Two Lightly brush the top side of the tuna steaks with a little more oil. Use a pair of tongs to turn over the tuna steaks, then season with salt and pepper. Continue grilling for an additional 2 minutes for rare or up to 4 minutes for well done. Let cool.

Three Meanwhile, bring a saucepan of salted water to a boil. Add the beans to the pan and return to a boil, then boil for 3 minutes, or until tender but crisp. Drain the beans and immediately transfer to a large bowl. Pour the garlic vinaigrette over the beans and stir together, then let the beans cool in the dressing.

four To serve, line a platter with lettuce leaves. Lift the beans out of the bowl, letting the excess dressing remain behind, and pile them in the center of the platter. Break the tuna into large flakes and arrange it over the beans.

five Arrange the hard-boiled eggs and tomatoes around the side. Place the anchovy fillets over the salad, then scatter with the olives. Drizzle any remaining dressing over the salad and serve.

Tapenade
Olive Spread

✤ Serves 8
✤ Prepared in
   15–20 minutes
✤ No cooking

4 cups ripe black olives, pitted
2 tablespoons capers
2 teaspoon Dijon mustard
juice of ½ lemon
1 garlic clove, finely chopped
12 canned anchovy fillets,
   drained and soaked to
   remove the salt
handful of chopped fresh
   flat-leaf parsley, plus sprigs
   to garnish
2 tablespoons chopped fresh
   thyme (optional)
⅔ cup extra virgin olive oil,
   plus extra for brushing
salt and pepper
slices of baguette or ciabatta,
   to serve

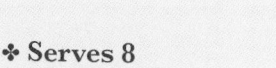
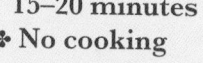

one

one

two

one Put all the ingredients except for the salt and pepper into a food processor and process until a good paste forms. Don't make it too smooth—it should retain a little coarseness.

Two Season with salt and pepper, keeping in mind that it may already be salty from the capers, olives, and anchovies. Brush slices of baguette with olive oil and toast them.

three Serve the tapenade with the slices of baguette and garnish with sprigs of parsley.

Soufflé au fromage
Cheese Soufflé

❖ Serves 4
❖ Prepared in 15 minutes
❖ Cooks in 30–35 minutes

1 tablespoon butter, melted
1 tablespoon finely grated Parmesan cheese
2 tablespoons butter
3 tablespoons all-purpose flour

1¼ cups whole milk
1 cup shredded cheddar cheese
1 teaspoon whole-grain mustard
grating of fresh nutmeg
4 extra-large eggs, separated
salt and pepper

one Preheat the oven to 400°F. Grease the bottom and sides of a soufflé dish with melted butter. Sprinkle the dish with the Parmesan cheese, turning the dish in your hands so that all the surface is covered with the cheese.

two Melt the remaining 2 tablespoons of butter in a saucepan (preferably nonstick) over medium heat. Add the flour, mix well using a wooden spoon, and cook for 1 minute, stirring continuously. Remove from the heat and stir in the milk gradually until you have a smooth consistency.

three Return the pan to low heat and continue to stir while the sauce comes to a boil and thickens. Simmer gently, stirring continuously, for about 3 minutes, or until the sauce is creamy and smooth. Remove from the heat and stir in the cheese, mustard, and nutmeg. Season well with salt and pepper. Set aside to cool a little. Whisk the egg whites until soft peaks have formed, but they are not too dry. Beat the egg yolks into the sauce mixture and then carefully stir in a little of the beaten egg white to slacken the mixture. Carefully fold in the remaining egg whites, then turn into the prepared dish. Place on a baking sheet and cook in the preheated oven for 25–30 minutes, or until well risen and golden brown. Serve immediately.

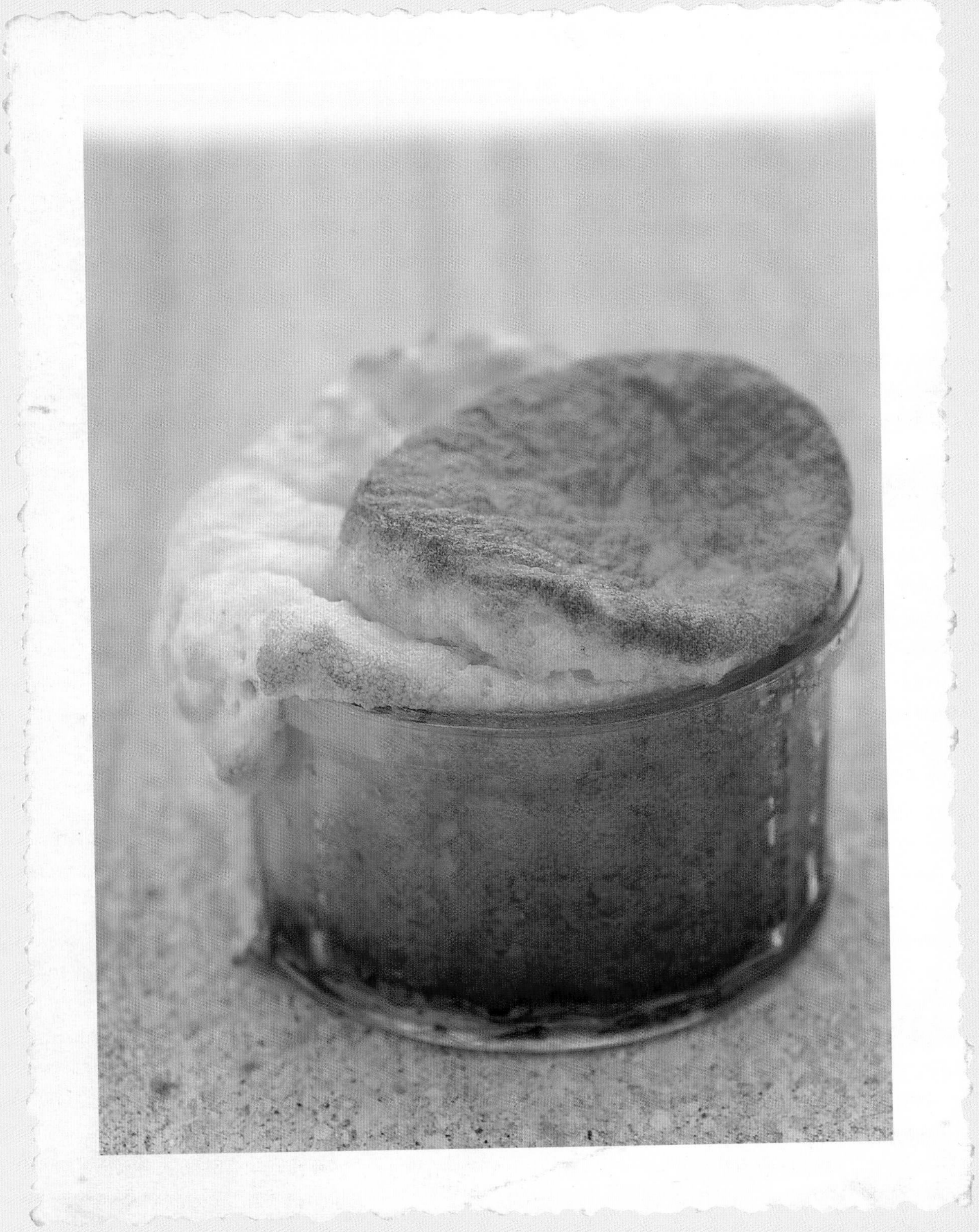

Asperges à la sauce hollandaise
Asparagus with Hollandaise Sauce

✤ Serves 4
✤ Prepared in
  10–15 minutes
✤ Cooks in 15–20 minutes

1½ pounds asparagus, trimmed

Hollandaise sauce
¼ cup white wine vinegar
½ tablespoon finely chopped
  shallots
5 black peppercorns
1 bay leaf
3 extra-large egg yolks
1¼ sticks unsalted butter,
  finely diced
2 teaspoons lemon juice
salt
pinch of cayenne pepper

one Divide the asparagus into four bundles and tie each with kitchen string, crisscrossing the string from just below the tips to the bottom. Stand the bundles upright in a deep saucepan. Add boiling water to come three-quarters of the way up the stems, then cover with a loose tent of aluminum foil, shiny-side down, inside the pan. Heat the water until bubbles appear around the side of the pan, then simmer for 10 minutes, or until the stems are just tender when pierced with the tip of a knife. Drain well.

Two Meanwhile, to make the hollandaise sauce, boil the vinegar, shallots, peppercorns, and bay leaf in a saucepan over high heat until reduced to 1 tablespoon. Cool slightly, then strain into a heatproof bowl that will fit over a saucepan of simmering water.

three Beat the egg yolks into the bowl. Set the bowl over the pan of simmering water and whisk the egg yolks continuously until they are thick enough to leave a trail on the surface.

four Do not let the water boil. Gradually beat in the butter, piece by piece, whisking continuously until the sauce is like soft mayonnaise. Stir in the lemon juice, then season with salt and cayenne pepper. Serve the sauce immediately with the asparagus.

one

Two

Three

23

chapter two

Meat & Poultry

Bœuf bourguignon

Steak frites

Croque-monsieur

Cassoulet

Navarin d'agneau

Gigot d'agneau aux haricots verts

Coq au vin

Confit de canard

Bœuf bourguignon
Beef Bourguignon

* ✤ Serves 6
* ✤ Prepared in 15–20 minutes
* ✤ Cooks in 3½ hours

2 tablespoons olive oil

6 ounces unsmoked bacon, sliced into thin strips

3 pounds boneless beef chuck or beef round, cut into 2-inch pieces

2 carrots, sliced

2 onions, chopped

2 garlic cloves, minced

3 tablespoons all-purpose flour

3 cups red wine

1½–2 cups beef stock

1 bouquet garni of 2 thyme sprigs, 2 parsley sprigs, and 3 bay leaves, tied with string

1 teaspoon salt

¼ teaspoon pepper

3 tablespoons butter

12 ounces pearl onions

3½ cups white button mushrooms

chopped fresh flat-leaf parsley, to garnish

mashed potatoes, to serve

one Heat the oil in a large casserole dish over medium heat. Add the bacon and brown for 2–3 minutes. Remove with a slotted spoon. Add the beef in batches to the dish and cook until browned. Drain and keep with the bacon. Add the carrots and chopped onions to the dish and cook for 5 minutes. Add the garlic and sauté until just golden. Return the meat and bacon to the casserole dish. Sprinkle the flour over the meat and cook for 1 minute, stirring. Add the wine, enough stock to cover, the bouquet garni, and the salt and pepper. Bring to a boil, cover, and simmer gently for 3 hours.

Two Heat half the butter in a skillet. Add the pearl onions, cover, and cook until softened. Remove with a slotted spoon and keep warm. Heat the remaining butter in the skillet. Add the mushrooms and sauté briefly. Set aside the mushrooms and keep warm.

three Remove the casserole dish from the heat and strain the casserole liquid through a strainer into a clean saucepan. Wipe the casserole dish with paper towels and transfer the meat mixture, mushrooms, and onions to the dish. Discard the bouquet garni. Remove the surface fat from the casserole liquid, simmer for 1–2 minutes to reduce, then pour it over the meat and vegetables in the dish. Serve immediately, garnished with parsley and with mashed potatoes on the side.

Steak frites
Steak & French Fries

✤ Serves 4
✤ Prepared in
   20–25 minutes
✤ Cooks in 45 minutes–
   1 hour

1 bunch of watercress, plus
   extra to garnish
6 tablespoons unsalted butter,
   softened
4 tenderloin steaks, about
   8 ounces each
4 teaspoons Tabasco sauce
salt and pepper

French Fries
4 potatoes, peeled
2 tablespoons sunflower oil

one To make the French fries, preheat the oven to 400°F. Cut the potatoes into thick, even-size sticks. Rinse them under cold running water, then dry well on a clean dish towel. Place in a bowl, add the oil, and toss together until coated.

Two Spread the potatoes on a baking sheet and cook in the preheated oven for 40–45 minutes, turning once, or until golden.

Three Using a sharp knife, finely chop enough watercress to fill ¼ cup. Place the butter in a small bowl and beat in the chopped watercress with a fork until completely incorporated. Cover with plastic wrap and let chill in the refrigerator until required.

four Preheat a ridged grill pan to high. Sprinkle each steak with 1 teaspoon of the Tabasco sauce, rubbing it in well. Season with salt and pepper.

five Cook the steaks on the preheated grill pan for 2½ minutes on each side for rare, 4 minutes on each side for medium, and 6 minutes on each side for well done. Transfer to serving plates and serve immediately, topped with the watercress butter and accompanied by the French fries. Garnish with watercress.

one

three

five

Croque-monsieur
Broiled Ham & Cheese Sandwich

✤ Serves 1
✤ Prepared in 5 minutes
✤ Cooks in 5–10 minutes

2 slices white bread, buttered
2 slices smoked ham
½ cup shredded Gruyère cheese or Swiss cheese
pat of butter, melted
salt and pepper
lightly dressed mixed green salad, to serve

one Preheat the broiler to high. Lay one piece of bread buttered side up and place the ham on top. Cover with two-thirds of the cheese and season with salt and pepper. Lay the other slice of bread on top, buttered side down. Brush the top side with the melted butter and place the bread, buttered side up, under the preheated broiler.

Two Broil until browned, then remove. Turn the sandwich over and scatter the remaining cheese on top. Replace under the broiler and cook until the cheese is bubbling and browned. Serve with a green salad.

Cassoulet

Pork & Lamb Casserole

✤ Serves 8
✤ Prepared in
   25–30 minutes,
   plus soaking
✤ Cooks in 3½ hours

2½ cups dried navy beans,
   soaked overnight
bouquet garni of 4 parsley
   sprigs, 2 thyme sprigs, and
   4 bay leaves, tied with string
1 celery stalk,
   coarsely chopped
3 onions, 1 quartered,
   2 thinly sliced
4 large garlic cloves,
   2 whole, 2 chopped
8¾ cups water
1 pound pork belly, skin
   removed and meat cut
   into 4 large chunks
1 pound shoulder of lamb,
   boned and cut into
   4 large chunks
2 tablespoons duck fat or
   vegetable oil
14 ounces Toulouse or pork
   sausage, sliced
7 ounces rindless smoked
   bacon, cut into thick strips
2 tablespoons tomato paste
3 cups fresh bread crumbs
salt and pepper

Two

Two

three

one Drain and rinse the beans and put them in a large saucepan with the bouquet garni, celery, onion quarters, and whole garlic and season with salt and pepper. Add the water and bring to a boil. Skim off any foam, then reduce the heat to low. Gently simmer for 1 hour, uncovered.

Two Meanwhile, cut the pork and lamb into pieces 1½ inches square, then add the duck fat to a large, heavy saucepan and put over high heat. Add the pork belly and brown it all over. Remove and reserve, then repeat with the sausage, then the lamb, then the bacon. Reserve the sausage, lamb and bacon. Add the sliced onions, chopped garlic, and tomato paste and cook in the remaining fat for 2 minutes. Remove from the heat and let cool.

three Preheat the oven to 350°F. Drain the beans, reserving the liquid but discarding the vegetables. In a large casserole dish, layer beans and meat alternately until they're all used. Add the garlic-and-tomato paste mixture and enough of the bean-cooking liquid to almost cover the beans. Sprinkle the bread crumbs over the beans and cook in the oven, covered, for 1 hour. Reduce the heat to 275°F, remove the cover, and cook for an additional hour.

four Check the casserole is not too dry, adding a little heated bean liquid or water, if necessary. Serve immediately.

Navarin d'agneau
Spring Lamb Stew

❖ Serves 4–6
❖ Prepared in 15–20 minutes
❖ Cooks in 1–1¼ hours

3 tablespoons butter
2 tablespoons sunflower oil, plus extra
   as needed
2 pounds boned shoulder of lamb,
   trimmed and cut into large chunks,
   any bones reserved
2 shallots, finely chopped
1 tablespoon sugar

4 cups lamb stock
2 tablespoons tomato paste
1 bouquet garni, with several parsley and
   thyme sprigs, 1 bay leaf, and 1 small
   rosemary sprig
8 new potatoes, scrubbed and halved, if large
4 young turnips, quartered
12 baby carrots, scrubbed
1 cup frozen peas
salt and pepper
chopped fresh flat-leaf parsley, to garnish

one Melt 2 tablespoons of the butter with the oil in a large skillet over medium heat. Add the lamb, in batches to avoid overcrowding the skillet, and cook, stirring, until browned on all sides, adding extra oil, if necessary. Transfer the meat to a casserole dish.

Two Melt the remaining butter with the fat left in the skillet. Add the shallots and stir for 3 minutes, or until beginning to soften. Sprinkle with the sugar, increase the heat, and continue stirring until the shallots caramelize, being careful that they do not burn. Transfer to the casserole dish and remove any charred sediment from the bottom of the skillet. Add half of the stock to the skillet and bring to a boil, scraping the bottom of the skillet, then tip this mixture into the casserole dish.

three Add the remaining stock, tomato paste, bouquet garni, and bones, if any, to the casserole dish. Season with salt and pepper. Cover and bring to a boil. Reduce the heat and simmer for 45 minutes.

Four Add the potatoes, turnips, and carrots and continue simmering for 15 minutes. Add the peas, then uncover and simmer for an additional 5–10 minutes, or until the meat and all the vegetables are tender. Remove and discard the bones, if used, and the bouquet garni. Taste and adjust the seasoning, if necessary. Garnish with parsley and serve.

Gigot d'agneau aux haricots verts
Roasted Leg of Lamb with Green Beans

* Serves 4–6
* Prepared in 10 minutes, plus marinating and resting
* Cooks in 1–1½ hours

3 garlic cloves, thinly sliced

1 leg of lamb, about 3 pounds

olive oil, for rubbing

½ cup dry red wine

½ cup water

2 tablespoons capers in brine, rinsed

3 cups green beans, trimmed

2 tablespoons butter

salt and pepper

one Make deep incisions all over the surface of the lamb. Push the garlic into the slits and then rub the leg all over with salt and pepper. Place the lamb in a roasting pan, rub all over with oil, and set aside for at least 1 hour for the garlic to penetrate.

Two Meanwhile, preheat the oven to 450°F. Calculate the roasting time at 15 minutes per 1 pound 2 ounces plus 15 minutes for medium, or plus 20 minutes for well done.

three Roast the lamb in the preheated oven for 10 minutes, then reduce the oven temperature to 350°F and continue roasting for the calculated roasting time, or until a meat thermometer reads about 130°F for medium-rare or 140°F for medium. Remove the lamb from the oven, transfer it to a carving dish, cover with a sheet of aluminum foil, and let rest for 20 minutes.

four While the lamb is resting, pour off any excess fat from the pan. Add the wine and water to the juices remaining in the pan and bring to a boil, scraping the sediment from bottom of the pan. Add the capers and heat through. Season this gravy with salt and pepper.

five Ten minutes before serving, bring a saucepan of lightly salted water to a boil. Add the beans, bring back to a boil, and cook for 5–8 minutes, or until tender. Drain well and return to the pan. Add the butter and season with salt and pepper.

six Carve the lamb and serve immediately with the green beans, alongside the gravy for spooning over the meat.

one

four

five

Coq au vin
Chicken in Wine

❖ Serves 4
❖ Prepared in 15–20 minutes
❖ Cooks in 1½ hours

4 tablespoons butter
2 tablespoons olive oil
4 pounds skinless, boneless chicken breasts
4 ounces rindless smoked bacon,
   cut into strips
4 ounces pearl onions

4 ounces cremini mushrooms, halved
2 garlic cloves, finely chopped
2 tablespoons brandy
1 cup red wine
1¼ cups chicken stock
1 bouquet garni of 2 thyme sprigs, 2 parsley
   sprigs, and 3 bay leaves, tied with string
2 tablespoons all-purpose flour
salt and pepper

one Melt half the butter with the olive oil in a large casserole dish. Add the chicken and cook over medium heat, stirring, for 8–10 minutes, or until golden brown all over. Add the bacon, onions, mushrooms, and garlic.

Two Pour in the brandy and set alight with a match. When the flames die down, add the wine, stock, and bouquet garni and season with salt and pepper. Bring to a boil, reduce the heat, and simmer gently for 1 hour, or until the chicken breasts are cooked all the way through and the juices run clear when the tip of a knife is inserted into the thickest part of the meat. Meanwhile, make a beurre manié (a butter-and-flour paste) by mashing the remaining butter with the flour in a bowl.

Three Discard the bouquet garni. Transfer the chicken to a large plate using a slotted spoon and keep warm. Slowly stir the beurre manié into the casserole dish. Bring to a boil, return the chicken to the dish, and serve immediately.

Confit de canard

Duck Confit

- ✤ Serves 4
- ✤ Prepared in 5 minutes, plus chilling and maturing
- ✤ Cooks in 3–4 hours

4 duck legs, about 10 ounces each
¼ cup coarse sea salt
1 teaspoon pepper
6 fresh thyme sprigs, chopped
4 fresh rosemary sprigs, chopped
2 bay leaves
5–6 cups duck fat, goose fat, or lard, plus extra, if necessary
sautéed potatoes and green salad, to serve

one Select one or two airtight, heatproof nonmetallic containers to store the duck legs in, and prepare this recipe at least eight days before you plan to use the duck legs. Rub each duck leg with the salt, then put them in the container or containers. Sprinkle with the pepper, thyme, and rosemary and tuck in the bay leaves. Cover tightly and refrigerate for at least 24 hours or for up to 48 hours.

Two To cook, preheat the oven to 250°F. Wipe the duck legs and discard the accumulated moisture and flavorings. Place the duck legs in a large casserole dish. Add the fat and heat until it melts. Cover the dish and transfer it to the oven for 3–4 hours, or until the duck legs have rendered their fat and are tender.

three Remove the legs and set aside. Strain the fat through a fine strainer. Pour a layer of the fat in the bottom of the container or containers and let set. Add the duck legs and pour enough fat over them to cover by at least 1 inch.

four Let the duck legs and fat cool, then cover and refrigerate for at least 1 week before using. When ready to use, place the container in simmering water to melt the fat. At this point the duck legs can be used in other recipes or cooked to serve with a salad. To cook, heat 2 tablespoons of the fat in a skillet over medium-high heat. Sauté the duck legs, skin side down, for 4–5 minutes, or until the skin browns. Turn them over and sauté on the other side for an additional 2 minutes. Serve immediately, with the potatoes and salad.

BRASSERIE
DE LA
CANCHE

Fish & Seafood

Tartare de saumon

Salmon Tartare

❖ Serves 4
❖ Prepared in
   25–30 minutes,
   plus chilling
❖ No cooking

1 pound salmon fillet, skinned
2 tablespoons sea salt
1 tablespoon sugar
2 tablespoons chopped
   fresh dill
1 tablespoon chopped
   fresh tarragon
1 teaspoon Dijon mustard
juice of 1 lemon
salt and pepper

Topping
1¾ cups cream cheese
1 tablespoon chopped fresh
   chives
pinch of paprika
snipped fresh dill and chives,
   to garnish

one

two

three

one Put the salmon into a shallow baking dish. Combine the sea salt, sugar, and dill, then rub the mixture into the fish until well coated. Season with plenty of pepper. Cover with plastic wrap and refrigerate for at least 48 hours, turning the salmon once.

Two When ready to serve, put the chopped tarragon into a mixing bowl with the mustard and lemon juice. Season well. Remove the salmon from the refrigerator, chop into small pieces, then add to the bowl. Stir until the salmon is well coated.

three To make the topping, put the cream cheese, chives, and paprika into a separate bowl and mix well. Place a 4-inch steel cooking ring or round pastry cutter on each of four small serving plates. Divide the salmon between the four steel rings so that each ring is filled halfway. Level the surface of each one, then top with the cream cheese mixture. Smooth the surfaces, then carefully remove the steel rings. Garnish with fresh dill and chives and serve immediately.

Sole meunière

Butter-Fried Sole

* Serves 2
* Prepared in 15–20 minutes
* Cooks in 15–20 minutes

4 sole fillets, about 6 ounces each, skinned
½ cup milk
¼ cup all-purpose flour

6 tablespoons butter
juice of ½ lemon
salt and pepper
chopped fresh flat-leaf parsley, to garnish
cooked asparagus and lemon
 wedges, to serve

one Rinse the fish under cold, running water and pat dry with paper towels. Pour the milk into a flat dish at least as large as the fillets and put the flour on a plate. Season each fillet on both sides with salt and pepper.

two Working with one fillet at a time, pull it quickly through the milk, then put it in the flour, turn once to coat all over, and shake off any excess flour. Continue until all the fillets are prepared.

three Melt half the butter in a sauté pan or skillet, large enough to hold the fillets in a single layer, over medium-high heat. Add the fillets to the pan, skinned-side down, and cook for 2 minutes.

four Turn over the fillets and cook for 2–3 minutes, or until the flesh flakes easily. Transfer to warm serving plates, skinned-side up, and set aside.

five Reduce the heat to medium and melt the remaining butter in the pan. When it stops foaming, add the lemon juice and stir, scraping the sediment from the bottom of the pan. Spoon the butter mixture over the fish and garnish with parsley. Serve with cooked asparagus and lemon wedges.

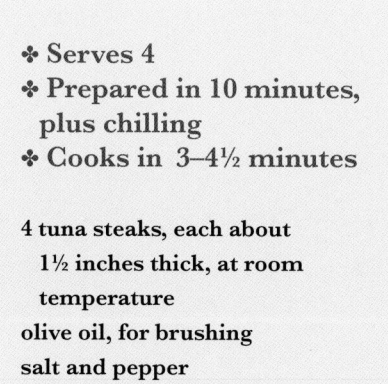

Steaks de Thon

Tuna Steaks

❖ Serves 4
❖ Prepared in 10 minutes, plus chilling
❖ Cooks in 3–4½ minutes

4 tuna steaks, each about
  1½ inches thick, at room
  temperature
olive oil, for brushing
salt and pepper
mixed salad greens, to serve

Mediterranean butter
1 garlic clove, finely chopped
1 stick butter, softened
2 tablespoons chopped
  fresh dill
4 ripe black olives in brine,
  drained, pitted and
  finely chopped
2 anchovy fillets in oil, drained
  and finely chopped
2 sun-dried tomatoes in oil,
  drained and finely chopped
finely grated rind of 1 lemon
pinch of cayenne pepper,
  or to taste
salt and pepper

one

Two

three

one At least 3 hours before you plan to cook, make the butter. Put the garlic clove on a cutting board and sprinkle with salt. Use the flat side of a knife to crush and scrape the garlic until a paste forms. Beat together the garlic, butter, dill, olives, anchovies, sun-dried tomatoes, lemon rind, and cayenne pepper in a bowl until all the ingredients are mixed. Season with salt and pepper.

Two Scrape the butter mixture onto a piece of wax paper and roll into a short log about 1 inch thick. Twist the ends of the paper to make a compact shape, then cut off any excess paper from one end. Stand the butter log upright in a glass and chill for at least 3 hours.

Three Heat a large, ridged grill pan over high heat. Brush the tuna with oil and season with salt and pepper on both sides. Place the tuna steaks in the pan and grill for 2 minutes. Brush the tuna with a little more oil, turn the steaks over, and continue cooking for an additional 1 minute for medium–rare or up to 2½ minutes for well done. Transfer the tuna steaks to plates and top each with a slice of the chilled butter. Serve immediately, with mixed salad greens.

Loup de mer frit

Pan-Fried Sea Bass

❖ Serves 4
❖ Prepared in 20–25 minutes
❖ Cooks in 35–40 minutes

7 potatoes (about 1¾ pounds), peeled and
   cut into chunks
6 whole garlic cloves, unpeeled
1 cup milk

½ cup heavy cream
4 tablespoons butter, diced
4 sea bass fillets, about 6 ounces,
   scaled but not skinned
3 tablespoons olive oil
salt and pepper
peas and lemon wedges, to serve

one Fill a large saucepan with cold water, add the potatoes and a generous pinch of salt, and bring to a boil. Simmer for 10–15 minutes, or until tender, then drain and return to the pan. Heat and stir for an additional 2 minutes to dry them out. Mash them using a potato ricer and set aside in the warm pan.

Two Bring a small saucepan of water to a boil, add the garlic, and blanch for 2 minutes, then drain and run under a little cold water. Peel off the skins and mash the garlic using a garlic crusher or the back of a spoon. Mix this into the potatoes. Put the milk in a saucepan and heat until hot but not boiling, then stir it into the potatoes, along with the cream. Heat over low heat for about 5 minutes, adding the butter a cube at a time. The potato should have a smooth consistency like a thick mayonnaise. Cover and keep warm.

three Carefully score the skin of the fish with a few diagonal cuts, being careful not to cut the flesh. Season with salt and pepper. Pour the oil into a large skillet and place over medium–high heat until shimmering. Cook the fillets, skin-side down, for 4 minutes. Check that the skin is crispy, then turn carefully and cook on the other side for just 1 minute. Spread some potato in the center of four warm plates and place a fish fillet on top, skin-side up. Serve with peas and lemon wedges.

Bouillinade

Fish & Potato Stew

❖ Serves 4
❖ Prepared in 5 minutes
❖ Cooks in 30–45 minutes

1½ tablespoons olive oil, plus
    extra for brushing
1 onion, finely chopped
3 large garlic cloves,
    2 chopped and 1 halved
1 tablespoon fennel seeds
½ teaspoon crushed red
    pepper, or to taste
pinch of saffron threads
1 (14½-ounce) can diced
    tomatoes
½ cup fish stock or water
2 bay leaves
4 Yukon gold or white round
    potatoes, thinly sliced
2 pounds mixed fish, such
    as hake, monkfish, and
    red snapper, skinned and
    cut into chunks
2 red bell peppers, seeded
    and sliced
2 tablespoons chopped fresh
    flat-leaf parsley
salt and pepper

one Preheat the oven to 350°F.

Two Heat the oil in a saucepan over medium heat. Add the onion and sauté, stirring, for 2 minutes. Add the chopped garlic, fennel seeds, crushed red pepper, and saffron and continue sautéing for an additional 1 minute, or until the onion is soft. Add the tomatoes, stock, and bay leaves and season with salt and pepper. Cover and bring to a boil, then reduce the heat to low and simmer for 10 minutes. Taste and adjust the seasoning, if necessary.

three Meanwhile, rub the garlic halves all over a 1½-quart baking dish, pressing down firmly, then set aside the dish, discarding the garlic cloves. Bring a large saucepan of lightly salted water to a boil, add the potatoes, bring back to a boil, and cook for 8–10 minutes, or until they are starting to soften but still hold their shape. Drain well, pat dry, and set aside.

four Place the prepared dish on a baking sheet and arrange half the potatoes in a layer at the bottom of the dish. Place the fish and red bell peppers on top. Spoon the tomato sauce over the fish, sprinkle with the parsley, and shake the dish slightly. Arrange the remaining potatoes on top to cover all the other ingredients and lightly brush with oil. Bake in the preheated oven for 20–25 minutes, or until the fish and potatoes are tender when pierced with a toothpick. Serve immediately.

Two

three

four

53

Moules marinières
Mussels in Wine

❖ Serves 4
❖ Prepared in 10–15 minutes
❖ Cooks in 10–15 minutes

4½ pounds mussels, scrubbed and debearded
1¼ cups dry white wine
6 shallots, finely chopped
bouquet garni of 2 thyme sprigs, 2 parsley sprigs,
   and 2 bay leaves, tied together with string
pepper
fresh flat-leaf parsley sprigs,
   to garnish
baguette, to serve

one Discard any mussels with broken shells and any that refuse to close when tapped.

Two Pour the wine into a large, heavy saucepan, add the shallots and bouquet garni, and season with pepper. Bring to a boil over medium heat, add the mussels, and cover tightly. Cook, shaking the saucepan occasionally, for 3–4 minutes, or until the mussels have opened. Remove and discard the bouquet garni and any mussels that remain closed.

three Using a slotted spoon, divide the mussels among individual serving dishes. Tilt the saucepan to let any sand settle, then spoon the cooking liquid over the mussels. Garnish with parsley sprigs and serve immediately with baguette.

Crevettes à la grecque

Shrimp in Mediterranean Sauce

✤ Serves 4
✤ Prepared in
   12–15 minutes, plus
   cooling and chilling
✤ Cooks in 30 minutes

½ cup dry white wine
½ cup water
⅓ cup olive oil
2 large garlic cloves,
   thinly sliced
1 small red onion,
   finely chopped
thinly pared zest of
   1 large lemon
2 tablespoons lemon juice
1 tablespoon coriander seeds,
   toasted and lightly crushed
½ tablespoon black or pink
   peppercorns, lightly crushed
pinch of crushed red pepper,
   or to taste
20 jumbo shrimp, peeled
   and deveined
salt and pepper
chopped fresh flat-leaf parsley,
   dill, or cilantro, to garnish
sliced baguette, to serve

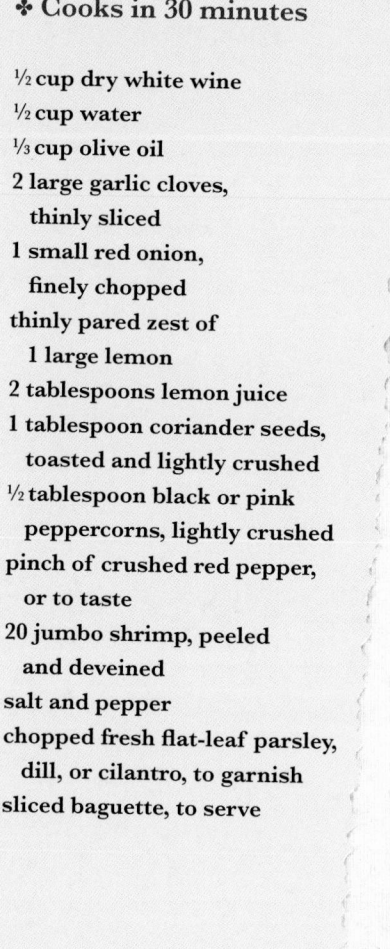

one

two

three

one Put the wine, water, oil, garlic, onion, lemon zest and juice, coriander seeds, peppercorns, and crushed red pepper into a saucepan. Cover and bring to a boil over high heat, then reduce the heat and simmer for 20 minutes.

Two Add the shrimp to the liquid and simmer for 2–3 minutes, or until they turn pink. Use a slotted spoon to remove the shrimp from the liquid immediately and transfer them to a deep bowl.

Three Bring the poaching liquid back to a boil, uncovered, and boil for 5 minutes, or until reduced by half. Let cool to lukewarm, then pour the liquid over the shrimp. Season the shrimp with salt and pepper and let cool completely. Cover the bowl with plastic wrap and chill for at least 4 hours.

four When ready to serve, garnish with parsley and serve chilled, with plenty of sliced baguette for mopping up the juices.

Bouillabaisse

Seafood Stew

✤ **Serves 8**
✤ **Prepared in 20–25 minutes**
✤ **Cooks in 50–55 minutes**

2¼ pounds of at least 4 different firm white fish fillets, such as red snapper, sea bass, rockfish, or monkfish, scaled and cleaned, but not skinned
½ cup olive oil
2 onions, finely chopped
1 fennel bulb, finely chopped
4 garlic cloves, crushed
3 (14½-ounce) cans diced tomatoes
6½ cups fish stock
pinch of saffron strands

grated zest of 1 orange
bouquet garni of 2 thyme sprigs, 2 parsley sprigs, and 2 bay leaves, tied together with string
1 pound mussels, scrubbed and debearded
1 pound cooked shrimp, shell on
salt and pepper
baguette, to serve

one Carefully pin bone the fish, then cut the fillets into bite-size pieces. Heat the olive oil in a large skillet or wide saucepan with a lid and gently sauté the onion and fennel for about 15 minutes, or until soft. Add the garlic and sauté for 2 minutes, then add the tomatoes and simmer for 2 minutes. Add the stock, saffron, orange zest, and bouquet garni and bring to a boil. Simmer, uncovered, for 15 minutes.

Two Discard any mussels with broken shells and any that refuse to close when tapped. Add the fish pieces, mussels, and shrimp and cover the skillet. Simmer for an additional 5–10 minutes, or until the mussels have opened. Discard any that remain closed. Season with salt and pepper.

Three Serve immediately with some crusty baguette.

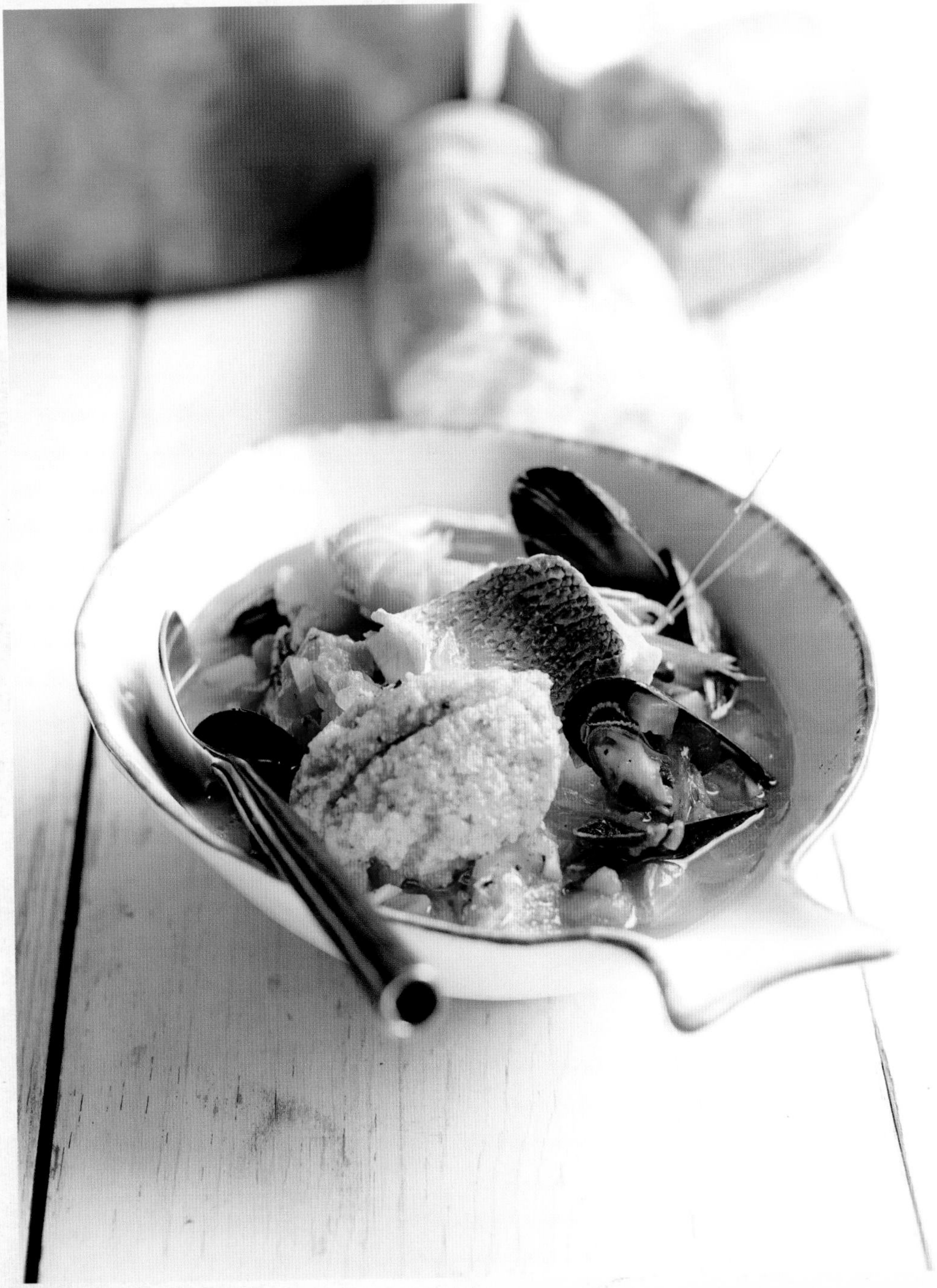

Vegetable Dishes

Ratatouille
Roasted Vegetables in Sauce

✤ **Serves 4**
✤ **Prepared in 20–25 minutes**
✤ **Cooks in 1½ hours**

3 red bell peppers
1 cup olive oil
1 zucchini, thickly sliced
1 fennel bulb, coarsely chopped
2 large red onions, thickly sliced

3 white onions, thickly sliced
2 large eggplants, thickly sliced
5 ripe tomatoes, blanched, peeled,
    cored, and seeded
1 heaped tablespoon fresh thyme leaves
1 heaped tablespoon fresh rosemary leaves
1 teaspoon sugar
salt and pepper

one Preheat the broiler to high, then place the red bell peppers on the broiler pan and place under the heat until the skin blackens. Turn and broil again, continuing until they are blackened all over. Put them in a bowl and cover with plastic wrap, let sweat for 10 minutes, then peel the bell peppers under cold running water. Cut them open and seed them, then chop the flesh into large chunks.

Two Meanwhile, place a large, heavy saucepan over medium heat and add half the oil. Add the zucchini and sauté until they begin to brown. Transfer to a large roasting pan and keep warm. Add the fennel and onions to the pan and sauté for 15–20 minutes, until they soften, then add them to the roasting pan. Add the eggplants and some more oil (they will soak up a lot) to the pan and cook until they begin to brown. Add them to the roasting pan, laid flat in a single layer.

Three Preheat the oven to 375°F. Add the tomatoes, red bell peppers, thyme, and rosemary to the roasting pan and distribute the vegetables evenly across it. Sprinkle the sugar over everything and gently mix through. There should be one layer of vegetables – if you need more room, use two roasting pans. Season with salt and pepper, drizzle with olive oil, and place, uncovered, in the preheated oven for 40–50 minutes, or until the vegetables start to brown.

four Refrigerate overnight or serve immediately.

Gratin de courgettes

Zucchini & Cheese Gratin

✤ Serves 4–6
✤ Prepared in
   25–30 minutes
✤ Cooks in 50–55 minutes

4 tablespoons butter, plus extra
   for greasing
6 zucchini, sliced
2 tablespoons chopped fresh
   tarragon or a mixture of
   fresh mint, tarragon, and
   flat-leaf parsley
2 cups grated Gruyère cheese
   or Parmesan cheese
½ cup milk
½ cup heavy cream
2 eggs, beaten
freshly grated nutmeg
salt and pepper

Two

three

four

one Preheat the oven to 350°F. Grease a large baking dish.

Two Melt the butter in a large sauté pan or skillet over medium–high heat. Add the zucchini and sauté for 4–6 minutes, turning the slices over occasionally, until browned on both sides. Remove from the pan and drain on paper towels, then season with salt and pepper.

Three Spread half the zucchini over the bottom of the prepared dish. Sprinkle with half the herbs and one-third of the cheese. Repeat these layers once again.

four Mix together the milk, cream, and eggs in a small bowl and season with nutmeg, salt, and pepper. Pour this liquid over the zucchini, then sprinkle the top with the remaining cheese.

five Bake in the preheated oven for 35–45 minutes, or until it is set in the center and golden brown. Remove from the oven and let stand for 5 minutes before serving straight from the dish.

Tarte à l'oignon
French Onion Tart

✤ **Serves 4**
✤ **Prepared in 20–25 minutes,**
 plus chilling
✤ **Cooks in 1¼ hours**

Pie dough
1⅔ cups all-purpose flour, plus extra to dust
pinch of salt
1 stick butter, plus extra for greasing
1 egg yolk

Filling
5 tablespoons butter
4 onions, thinly sliced
2 teaspoons thyme leaves
2 eggs
1 cup heavy cream
½ cup shredded Gruyère cheese
½ teaspoon fresh grated nutmeg
salt and pepper

one Preheat the oven to 350°F and grease an 8-inch loose-bottom tart pan. To make the dough, sift the flour and salt together into a large bowl, dice the butter and add to the bowl, then rub with your fingers until the mixture resembles fine bread crumbs. Add the egg yolk and just enough water to bind to a soft, but not sticky, dough. Roll into a ball, wrap in plastic wrap, and refrigerate for 15 minutes before using.

Two Roll out the dough on a lightly floured surface. Press the dough into the prepared tart pan, lay a piece of parchment paper on it, fill with pie weights or dried beans, and bake in the preheated oven for 15 minutes. Remove from the oven and increase the oven temperature to 400°F. Remove the paper and weights and bake the pastry shell for an additional 5 minutes. Keep the oven on.

three To make the filling, melt the butter in a large, heavy skillet over medium–low heat, add the onions and thyme, and cook gently, stirring frequently, for 15–30 minutes, until lightly browned. Season with salt and pepper, remove from the heat, and let cool for 10 minutes.

four Lower the oven temperature to 375°F. In a large bowl, beat together the eggs and cream. Add the cheese, nutmeg, and cooked onion mixture and stir. Pour the mixture into the pastry shell and bake, uncovered, for 30–40 minutes, or until golden brown. Serve immediately.

Tarte aux Tomates

Tomato Tart

✤ Serves 4
✤ Prepared in
   20–25 minutes
✤ Cooks in 40–45 minutes

Pie dough
2 cups all-purpose flour
pinch of salt
1¼ sticks butter
1 tablespoon chopped oregano,
   plus extra to garnish
about ⅓ cup cold water

Filling
2 tablespoons butter
1 tablespoon sugar
9 small tomatoes, halved
1 garlic clove, crushed
2 teaspoons white wine vinegar
salt and pepper

one

three

three

one Preheat the oven to 400°F. To make the filling, melt the butter in a heavy saucepan. Add the sugar and stir over high heat until just turning golden brown. Remove from the heat and quickly add the tomatoes, garlic, and white wine vinegar, stirring to coat evenly. Season with salt and pepper.

two Transfer the tomatoes to a 9-inch cake pan, spreading them evenly, cut side down.

three To make the dough, place the flour, salt, butter, and oregano in a food processor and process until the mixture resembles fine bread crumbs. Add just enough water to bind to a soft, but not sticky, dough. Roll out the dough to a 10-inch circle and place it over the tomatoes, tucking in the edges. Pierce with a fork to let out steam.

four Bake in the preheated oven for 25–30 minutes, or until firm and golden. Rest for 2–3 minutes, then run a knife around the edge and turn out onto a warm serving plate.

five Sprinkle the tart with chopped oregano, and serve immediately.

Aumonières de poireaux
Leek Crepes

❖ **Makes 8**
❖ **Prepared in 20–25 minutes**
❖ **Cooks in 35 minutes**

Filling
2 tablespoons unsalted butter
½ tablespoon sunflower oil
2 leeks, finely shredded
freshly grated nutmeg, to taste
1 tablespoon finely snipped fresh chives
3 ounces soft goat cheese,
   rind removed if necessary, chopped
salt and pepper

Crepes
1¼ cups all-purpose flour
pinch of salt
1 cup whole milk
1 extra-large egg
2 tablespoons melted butter
butter, for cooking

one Preheat the oven to 400°F. To make the filling, melt the butter with the oil in a skillet with a lid over medium–high heat. Add the leeks and stir so that they are well coated. Season with salt and pepper, but remember the cheese might be salty. Add a few gratings of nutmeg, then cover the leeks with a sheet of wet wax paper and put the lid on the skillet. Reduce the heat to low and let the leeks sweat for 5–7 minutes, or until tender but not brown. Stir in the chives, then check the seasoning.

Two To make the crepes, sift the flour and salt into a bowl. Add the milk, egg, and melted butter and beat to a smooth batter. Let stand for 15 minutes. Heat the butter in a large skillet. Pour in just enough batter to cover the skillet, swirling to create a thin layer. Cook until the underside is golden, then flip and cook the other side. Repeat with the remaining batter until you have eight crepes.

Three Put one crepe on the work surface and put one-eighth of the leeks on the crepe, top with one-eighth of the cheese, then fold the crepe into a square package or simply roll it around the filling. Place the stuffed crepe on a baking sheet, then continue to fill and fold or roll the remaining crepes. Put the baking sheet in the preheated oven and bake for 5 minutes, or until the crepes are hot and the cheese starts to melt. Serve immediately.

Clafoutis au fromage
Cheese Clafoutis

✤ Serves 4–6
✤ Prepared in 15 minutes
✤ Cooks in 50–55 minutes

olive oil, for greasing
3 cups cherry tomatoes
3 ounces goat cheese, rind removed if necessary, finely crumbled
2 tablespoons fresh thyme leaves
½ cup all-purpose flour
pinch of sugar
4 extra-large eggs
1¼ cups whole milk
salt

one

Two

Three

one Preheat the oven to 350°F. Lightly grease a 1½-quart baking dish. Arrange the tomatoes in a single layer in the dish, then scatter the cheese and thyme over them and set aside.

Two Sift the flour, sugar, and a pinch of salt into a large bowl and make a well in the center. Break the eggs into the well and use a whisk or fork to blend them together. Add half the milk and stir, gradually incorporating the flour from the side of the bowl until blended. Stir in the remaining milk until a smooth batter forms.

three Gently pour the batter over the tomatoes, shaking the dish slightly to distribute the cheese and thyme. Place in the preheated oven and bake for 50–55 minutes, or until the batter is puffed, golden, and set and the tomatoes are tender.

four Remove the clafoutis from the oven and let stand for 5 minutes before serving.

Artichauts entiers
Whole Artichokes

✤ Serves 4
✤ Prepared in 20–25 minutes,
 plus cooling
✤ Cooks in 40–45 minutes

2 lemons
4 large globe artichokes
2¼ sticks butter
2 tablespoons fresh thyme leaves
zest and juice of 1 lemon
salt and pepper
crusty bread, to serve

one Fill a large saucepan halfway with cold water. Halve the lemons, squeeze the juice into the water, and drop the skins in, too. Cut the stems off the artichokes near the bottom, then chop off the top 1 inch of the leaves. Add them to the water, cover, and bring to a boil. Once boiling, the artichokes will take 20–30 minutes to cook, depending on their tenderness and size. They are ready when the outer leaves can be pulled off without any effort.

Two Drain the artichokes, turn them upside down, and let cool for 15 minutes while you make the lemon-and-thyme-flavored butter. Gently melt the butter in a small saucepan, then mix in the thyme, lemon zest and juice, and salt and pepper.

three Place the artichokes in four shallow dishes, seasoned with salt and pepper. Serve the butter in small bowls and place a large bowl in the middle of the table for discarded artichoke pieces and leaves.

Omelette aux fines herbes
Mixed Herb Omelet

❖ Serves 1
❖ Prepared in 10 minutes
❖ Cooks in 15–20 minutes

2 extra-large eggs
2 tablespoons milk
3 tablespoons butter
leaves from 1 fresh flat-leaf
   parsley sprig, plus extra
   to garnish
1 fresh chervil sprig, chopped,
   plus extra to garnish
2 fresh chives, snipped, plus
   extra to garnish
salt and pepper

one Break the eggs into a bowl. Add the milk, season with salt and pepper, and quickly beat until just blended.

Two Heat an 8-inch omelet pan or skillet over medium-high heat until hot and you can feel the heat rising from the surface. Add 2 tablespoons of the butter and use a fork to rub it over the bottom and around the sides as it melts.

three As soon as the butter stops sizzling, pour in the eggs. Shake the pan back and forth over the heat and use the fork to stir the eggs around the pan in a circular motion. Do not scrape the bottom of the pan.

four As the omelet begins to set, use the fork to push the cooked egg from the edge toward the center, so the remaining uncooked egg comes in contact with the hot bottom of the pan. Continue doing this for 3 minutes, or until the omelet looks set on the bottom but is still slightly runny on top.

five Place the herbs in the center of the omelet. Tilt the pan away from the handle, so the omelet slides toward the edge of the pan. Use the fork to fold the top part of the omelet over the herbs and then fold over the bottom part. Slide the omelet onto a plate, then rub the remaining butter over the top. Serve immediately.

one

four

five

chapter five

Desserts

Crème brûlée

Crème brûlée

* Serves 6
* Prepared in 20–25 minutes
* Cooks in 1 hour

2 cups heavy cream
1 vanilla bean
½ cup superfine sugar, plus extra
   for the topping
6 egg yolks

one Preheat the oven to 325°F.

two Pour the cream into a small saucepan. Split the vanilla bean in half lengthwise. Scrape the seeds into the pan, then chop the bean into little pieces and add it, too. Heat the cream to boiling, then reduce the heat and simmer gently for 5 minutes.

three Put the sugar and egg yolks in a heatproof bowl and beat with a spoon until well mixed. Pour the hot cream into the egg mixture, beating (not whisking) as you pour, until it has thickened. Pass this custard through a fine strainer into another bowl. Pour the mixture into a wide, flat dish and lay it in a roasting pan. Boil a saucepan of water and carefully pour the hot water into the pan so that it comes halfway up the sides of the crème brûlée dish.

four Place in the preheated oven and bake for about 30–45 minutes, or until the custard has just set.

five Remove from the oven and let cool to room temperature. Sprinkle a little superfine sugar over the custard, then gently caramelize it using a kitchen blow torch or by putting it under a hot broiler. Let cool for a few minutes, then serve.

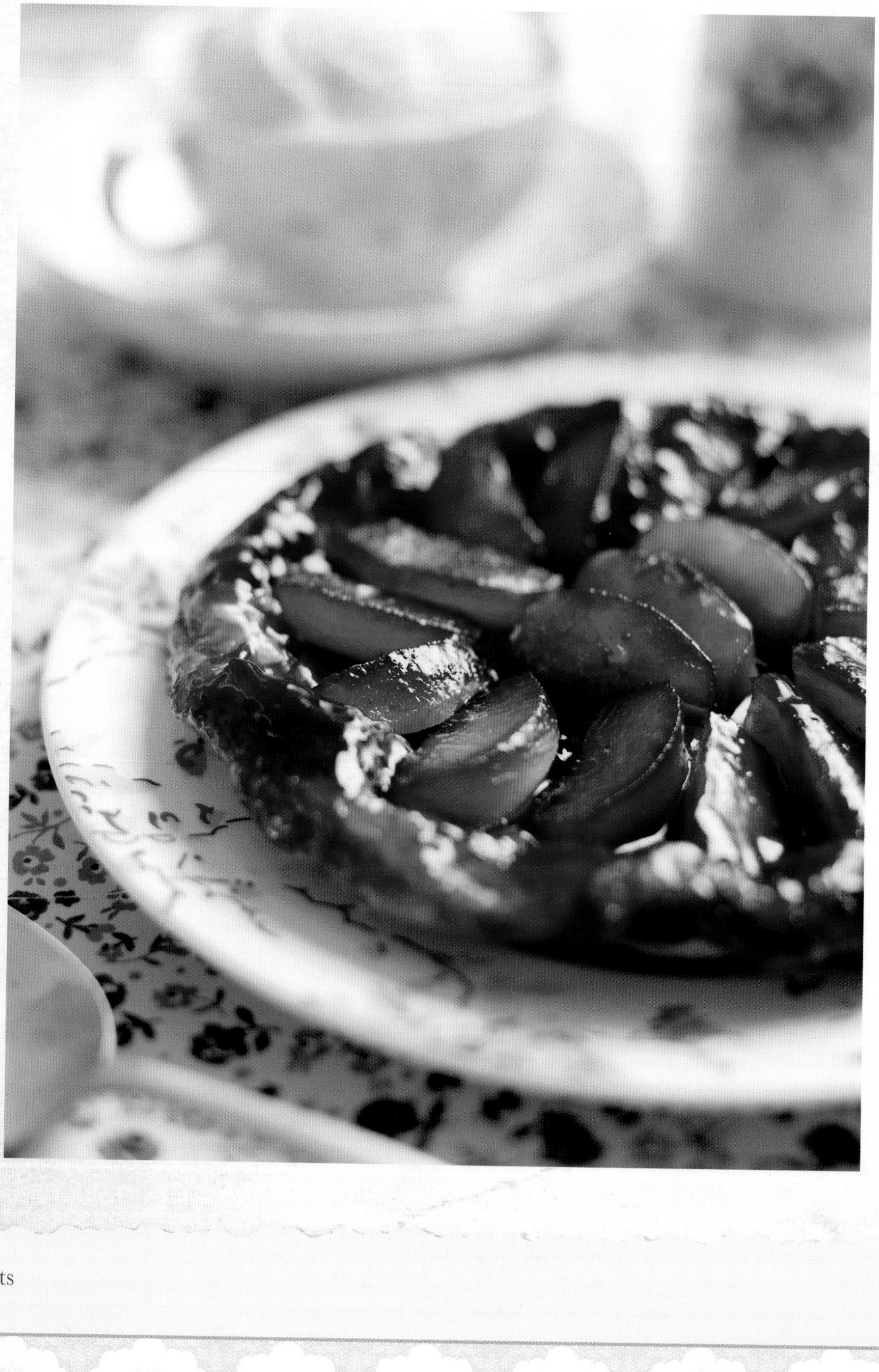

Tarte Tatin

Apple Tart

* Serves 6
* Prepared in 25–30 minutes,
  plus resting
* Cooks in 45–50 minutes

1 cup superfine sugar
1¼ sticks unsalted butter
4 Pippin or Golden Delicious apples, peeled,
   cored, and sliced
1 sheet ready-to-bake puff pastry
all-purpose flour, for dusting
vanilla ice cream, to serve (optional)

one Place an 8-inch ovenproof skillet over low heat and add the sugar. Melt the sugar until it starts to caramelize, but do not let it burn, then add the butter and stir it in to make a light toffee sauce. Remove from the heat.

Two Place the apple slices in the skillet on top of the toffee sauce. The apples should fill the skillet. Put the skillet over medium heat and cover. Simmer, without stirring, for about 5–10 minutes, until the apples soak up some of the sauce, then remove from the heat.

Three Preheat the oven to 375°F. Roll out the pastry on a lightly floured surface, making sure it is large enough to thickly cover the skillet with extra space on the sides. Lay it on top of the apples and tuck the edges down between the fruit and skillet until it is sealed. Don't worry about making it look too neat—it will be turned over before eating.

four Put the skillet into the preheated oven and bake for 25–35 minutes, checking to make sure the pastry doesn't burn. The pastry should be puffed and golden. Remove from the oven and let rest for 30–60 minutes.

five When you're ready to eat, make sure the tart is still a little warm (reheat it on the stove, if necessary) and place a plate on top. Carefully invert it and lift the skillet off. Serve with some vanilla ice cream, if using.

Macarons à la vanille
Vanilla Macaroons

✤ **Makes 16**
✤ **Prepared in 30 minutes, plus resting**
✤ **Cooks in 10–15 minutes**

¾ cup almond meal
  (ground almonds)
1 cup confectioners' sugar
2 extra-large egg whites
¼ cup superfine sugar
½ teaspoon vanilla extract

Filling
4 tablespoons unsalted butter,
  softened
½ teaspoon vanilla extract
1 cup confectioners' sugar,
  sifted

three

four

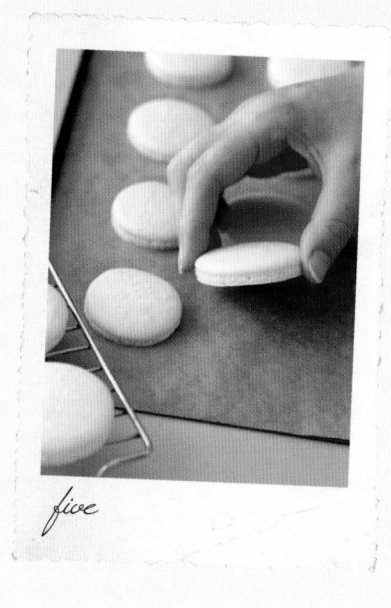

five

one Place the almond meal and confectioners' sugar in a food processor and process for 15 seconds. Sift the mixture into a bowl. Line two baking sheets with parchment paper.

Two Place the egg whites in a large bowl and beat until holding soft peaks. Gradually beat in the superfine sugar to make a firm, glossy meringue. Beat in the vanilla extract.

three Using a spatula, fold the almond mixture into the meringue, one-third at a time. When all the dry ingredients are thoroughly incorporated, continue to cut and fold the mixture until it forms a shiny batter with a thick, ribbonlike consistency.

four Pour the mixture into a pastry bag fitted with a ½-inch plain tip. Pipe 32 small circles onto the prepared baking sheets. Tap the baking sheets firmly onto a work surface to remove air bubbles. Let stand at room temperature for 30 minutes. Meanwhile, preheat the oven to 325°F.

five Bake in the preheated oven for 10–15 minutes. Let cool for 10 minutes, carefully peel the macaroons off the parchment paper, then let cool completely.

six To make the filling, beat the butter and vanilla extract in a bowl until pale and fluffy. Gradually beat in the confectioners' sugar until smooth and creamy. Use to sandwich pairs of macaroons together.

Clafoutis aux myrtilles
Blueberry Clafoutis

✤ **Serves 4**
✤ **Prepared in 15–20 minutes**
✤ **Cooks in 30 minutes**

2 tablespoons butter, softened,
   plus extra for greasing
$\frac{2}{3}$ cup superfine sugar
3 eggs
$\frac{1}{2}$ cup all-purpose flour
1 cup light cream
$\frac{1}{2}$ teaspoon ground cinnamon
3 cups blueberries
confectioners' sugar, for dusting

one Preheat the oven to 350°F. Grease a 1-quart baking dish.

two Put the butter in a bowl with the superfine sugar and beat together until pale and creamy. Add the eggs and beat together well. Sift in the flour, then gradually stir in the cream, followed by the cinnamon. Continue to stir until smooth.

three Arrange the blueberries in the bottom of the prepared baking dish, then pour the batter over the berries. Transfer to the preheated oven and bake for about 30 minutes, or until puffed and golden.

four Remove from the oven, dust lightly with confectioners' sugar, and serve.

Parfait à la framboise
Raspberry Parfait

- ✤ Serves 6
- ✤ Prepared in 15 minutes, plus freezing
- ✤ Cooks in 10 minutes

3½ cups raspberries, plus extra to decorate

⅔ cup confectioners' sugar

1 tablespoon kirsch or cherry brandy (optional)

⅓ cup granulated sugar

½ cup water

2 egg whites

1¼ cups heavy whipping cream

one Put the raspberries in a food processor or blender and process to form a smooth puree. Push through a nylon strainer into a bowl to remove the seeds.

Two Sift the confectioners' sugar into the raspberry puree, then stir together until well mixed. Stir in the kirsch or cherry brandy, if using.

Three Put the granulated sugar and water in a small, heavy saucepan over low heat and heat gently, stirring, until the sugar has dissolved. Bring to a boil, then boil, without stirring, for 5 minutes, or until a syrup has formed. Do not let it brown. Meanwhile, beat the egg whites in a large bowl until stiff and dry.

four Drizzle the hot sugar syrup in a thin stream onto the beaten egg whites, beating all the time until the mixture is thick, creamy, and fluffy. Continue beating until the mixture is cold.

five Whip the cream until stiff. Fold the raspberry puree into the egg white mixture, then fold in the whipped cream.

six Freeze the raspberry mixture in a freezerproof container, uncovered, for 1–2 hours, or until mushy. Turn the mixture into a bowl and stir vigorously to break down any ice crystals. Return to the container and freeze for an additional 1–2 hours, or until firm. Cover the container with a lid for storing. Serve in sundae dishes, sprinkled with raspberries.

Two

three

five

Tarte au citron
Lemon Tart

✤ **Serves 6–8**
✤ **Prepared in 25 minutes, plus chilling**
✤ **Cooks in 35 minutes**

grated rind of 2–3 large lemons
²/₃ cup lemon juice
½ cup superfine sugar
½ cup heavy cream or crème fraîche
3 extra-large eggs
3 extra-large egg yolks
confectioners' sugar, for dusting
fresh raspberries, to serve

Pie dough
1⅓ cups plus 1 tablespoon all-purpose flour, plus extra for dusting
½ teaspoon salt
1 stick unsalted butter, chilled and diced
1 egg yolk, beaten with 2 tablespoons ice-cold water

one To make the dough, sift the flour and salt into a large bowl. Add the butter and rub it in with your fingertips until the mixture resembles fine bread crumbs. Add the egg yolk and water and mix to form a dough. Gather the dough into a ball, wrap in plastic wrap, and let chill for at least 1 hour.

two Preheat the oven to 400°F. Roll the dough out on a lightly floured surface and use to line a 9–10-inch loose-bottom tart pan. Prick the bottom of the dough all over with a fork and line with parchment paper and pie weights or dried beans.

three Bake in the preheated oven for 15 minutes, or until the pastry looks set. Remove the paper and weights. Reduce the oven temperature to 375°F.

four Beat together the lemon rind, lemon juice, and superfine sugar until blended. Slowly beat in the cream, then beat in the eggs and yolks, one by one.

five Place the pastry shell on a baking sheet and pour in the filling. Transfer to the preheated oven and bake for 20 minutes, or until the filling is set.

six Let cool completely on a wire rack. Dust with confectioners' sugar and serve with raspberries.

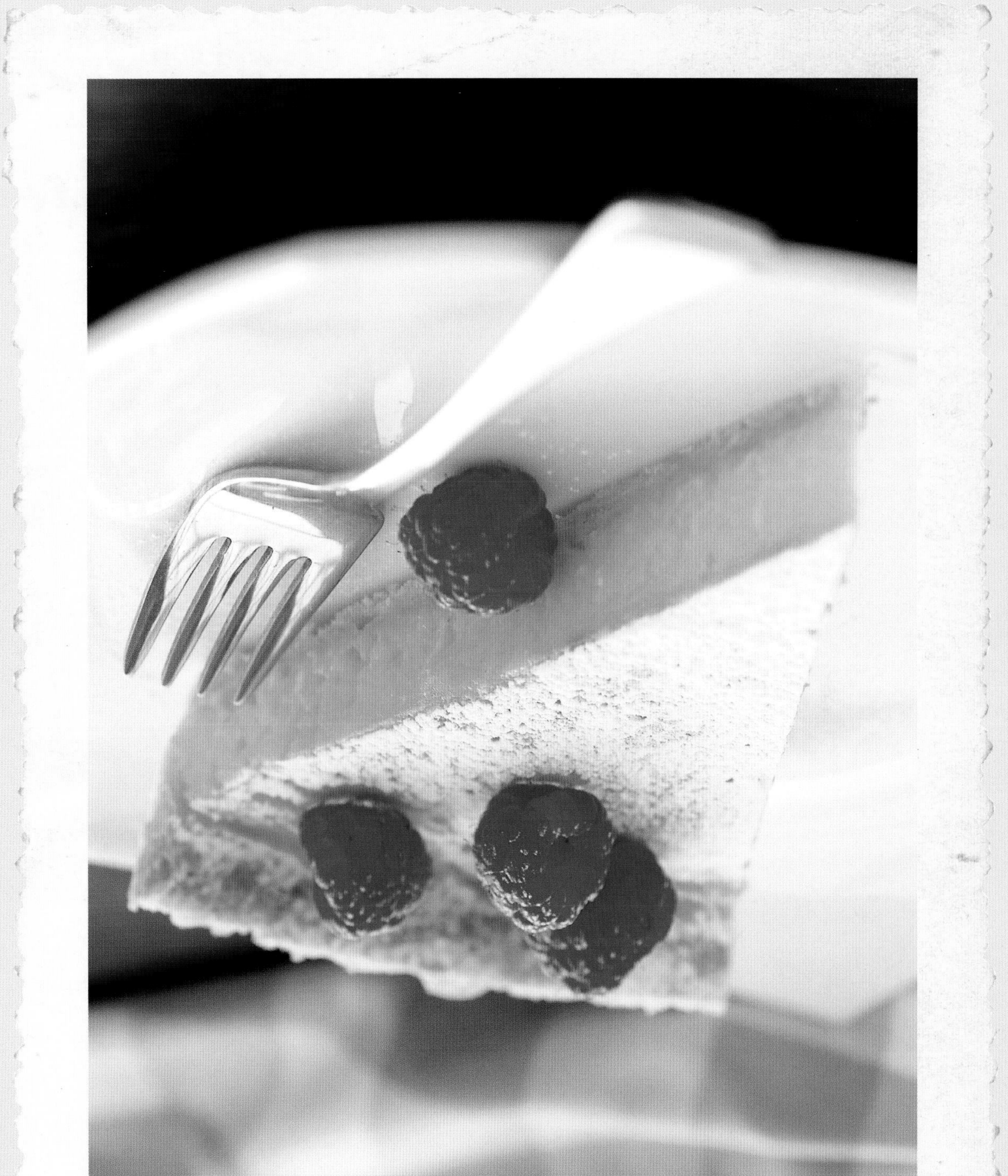

Mousse au chocolat

Chocolate Mousse

❖ **Serves 4–6**
❖ **Prepared in 10 minutes, plus chilling**
❖ **Cooks in 6–10 minutes**

10 ounces semisweet dark chocolate, broken into small pieces, plus extra finely chopped pieces, to serve
1½ tablespoons unsalted butter
1 tablespoon brandy
4 eggs, separated

one

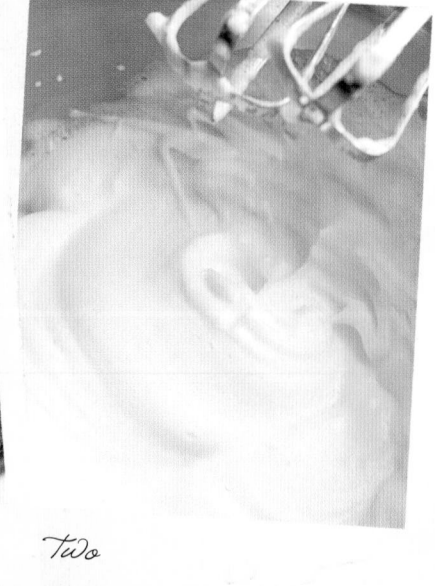

Two

one Place the chocolate in a heatproof bowl set over a saucepan of gently simmering water. Add the butter and melt with the chocolate, stirring, until smooth. Remove from the heat, stir in the brandy, and let cool slightly. Add the egg yolks and beat until smooth.

Two In a separate bowl, beat the egg whites until stiff peaks form, then fold into the chocolate mixture. Spoon into small serving bowls or custard cups and level the surfaces. Transfer to the refrigerator and chill for at least 4 hours, or until set.

three Take the mousse out of the refrigerator and serve, sprinkled with finely chopped chocolate pieces.

Two

Profiteroles

Profiteroles

* Serves 4
* Prepared in 25–35 minutes
* Cooks in 40–45 minutes

Choux pastry dough
5 tablespoons unsalted butter,
    plus extra for greasing
1 cup water
¾ cup all-purpose flour
3 eggs, beaten

Cream filling
1¼ cups heavy cream
3 tablespoons superfine sugar
1 teaspoon vanilla extract

Chocolate sauce
4 ounces semisweet dark chocolate,
    broken into small pieces
2½ tablespoons unsalted butter
⅓ cup water
2 tablespoons brandy (optional)

one Preheat the oven to 400°F. Grease a large baking sheet.

two To make the pastry dough, place the butter and water in a saucepan and bring to a boil. Meanwhile, sift the flour into a bowl. Turn off the heat and beat the flour into the butter mixture until smooth. Let cool for 5 minutes. Beat in enough of the eggs to give the mixture a soft, dropping consistency.

three Transfer the mixture to a pastry bag fitted with a ½-inch plain tip. Pipe small balls onto the prepared baking sheet. Bake in the preheated oven for 25 minutes. Remove from the oven. Pierce each ball with a toothpick to let the steam escape.

four To make the filling, whip together the cream, sugar, and vanilla extract in a small bowl. Cut the pastry balls across the middle, then pipe the filling into the balls.

five To make the sauce, gently melt together the chocolate, butter, and water in a small saucepan, stirring continuously, until smooth. Stir in the brandy, if using.

six Pile the profiteroles into individual serving dishes, pour the sauce over them, and serve immediately.

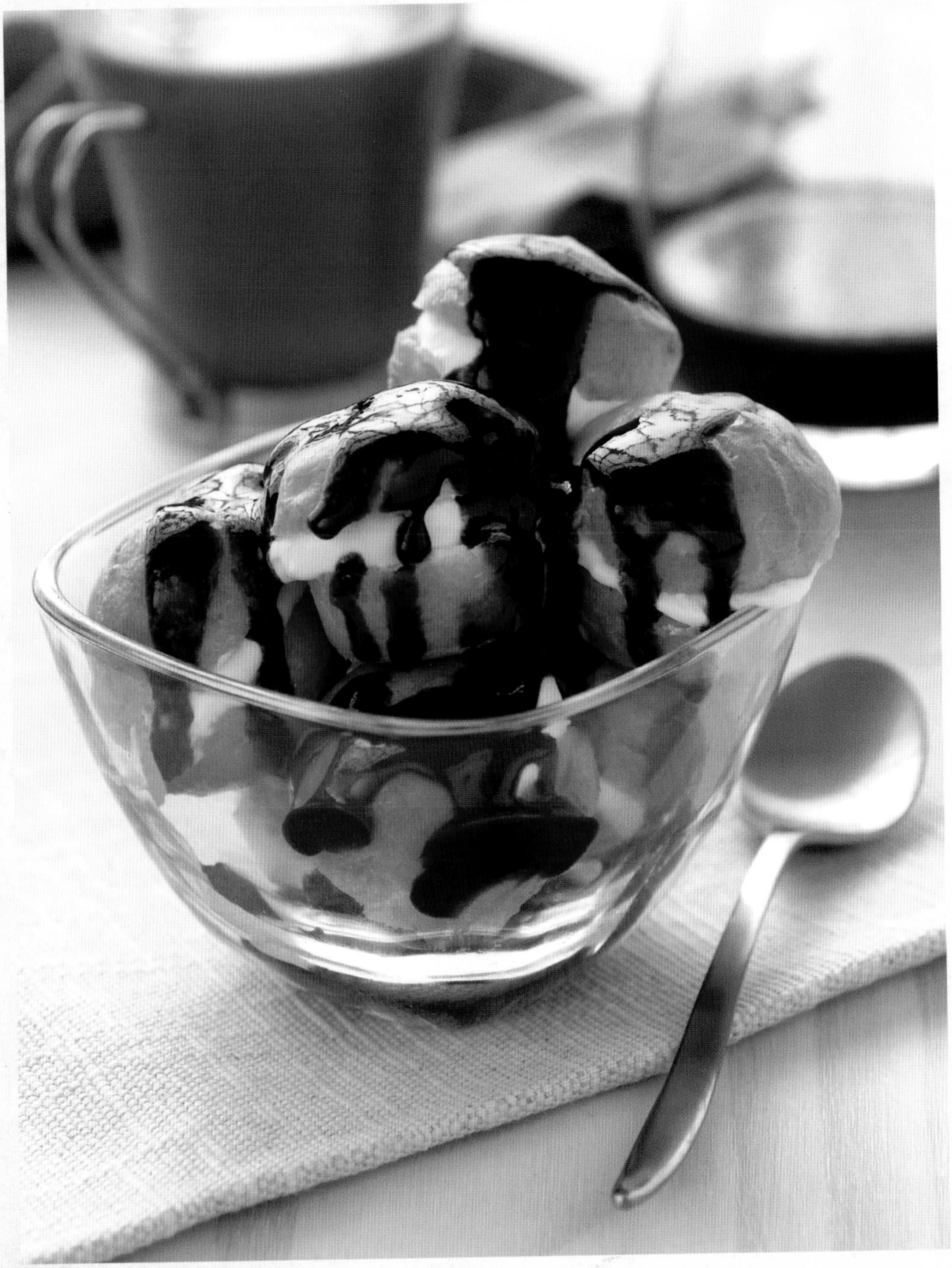